Contents

RICH
ON ANY
ALLOWANCE

*The Easy Budgeting
System for
Kids and Teens*

James P. Christensen and Clint Combs
with Philip D. Thorpe

SHADOW MOUNTAIN

Salt Lake City, Utah

Shadow Mountain is an imprint of Deseret Book Company,
P.O. Box 30178, Salt Lake City, Utah 84130.

ISBN 0-87579-065-8
Library of Congress Catalog Card Number 86-72093

First printing November 1986

Illustrations in chapter 1 by Shauna Gillette, except
illustration of Shauna by David Jensen.

A Note to Parents

Our business is helping people prevent or solve their financial problems and improve their overall financial situation. Almost always, financial problems have little to do with how much money is earned but much to do with how it is managed. Consequently, we developed the Financial Freedom Budget System.

In private counseling and seminars with couples and individuals throughout the country, and in our first book, we have concentrated on adults. In this book, we focus our attention and experience on that previously neglected but deserving segment of the population—the young people. For them, we have developed the Financial Freedom *Junior* Budget System.

As parents, we don't leave to chance the teaching of our children how to read, write, and do arithmetic; how to drive a car; or anything else of lifelong importance. Neither should we leave to chance the teaching of our children how to properly handle their money, one of life's most enduring challenges.

People's attitudes about money and their habits in handling it are learned from two main sources: the example set by their parents, and their own experiences with it during their formative years. It is easier for people to learn most things when they are young. To learn or relearn something when they are older takes more time and effort. And much of that late learning or relearning comes after some costly mistakes.

That leads to the question frequently asked us: At what age should young people begin using this system? They could begin using it as soon as they are able to print numbers. We recommend, however, that they start by at least age eight. In most cases, they will graduate from this junior system when they open a checking account *and* obtain a credit card. When they reach that point, we recommend that they read our first book, *Rich on Any Income*, which goes beyond this book in teaching them how to use a checking account and credit card along with the Financial Freedom Budget System.

We find that if adults do not manage their money carefully and wisely, they develop financial problems that usually lead to unhappiness. The same is true for children. Have you ever seen the sadness in children's eyes when their little nest egg, which they have worked so hard to save, vanishes from mismanagement? Or have you seen their frustration at not being able to save at all? Ask any parent what their main goal for their children is, and they will almost always reply that they want them to be happy. Teaching children how to manage their money is one way parents can help bring about that happiness for their children, now and in the future.

It is important that you give your children some kind of allowance, not so that they will have money, but so that they will have money to *manage* as they learn the skills taught in this book. This small investment on your part will pay huge dividends for them throughout their lives.

Based on the success that we have had in teaching our budget system through our counseling, through our book *Rich on Any Income,* and through our Financial Freedom Budget Seminar, to over 60,000 people from all walks of life, including children, we can make this bold promise to young people: If they will faithfully follow the principles and procedures in this book, they will have the joy and peace that come from financial freedom and security. Also, they can have more of anything they want financially as long as they plan and work for it over time.

In this book, young people will learn to establish spending goals, save money regularly, limit impulse spending, live within their means, and avoid overextending themselves in debt. It doesn't matter whether their income is regular or sporadic; big or little; or from allowances, gifts, odd jobs, or part- or full-time employment. What does matter is that they will learn to manage their money successfully. Also, they will learn how to prepare for a checking account and credit card. And they will have fun doing it!

Parents often ask us, "How can I best use your book to teach my children to budget their money?"

As you read or skim through this book, you will note that it is generally written at a level that teenagers will understand. However, if you have children who are not yet teenagers but who are old enough to do simple addition and subtraction, this book is for them, too. In their case, however, you will need to read the book yourself and then teach them to use the parts of the budgeting system they need in a way they will understand.

We have found that children's ages are not directly related to their financial needs. Eight- or nine-year-olds often have passbook savings accounts and want to learn how to spend from them. But even children in their late teens often have passbook savings accounts and need to know how to use them in budgeting their money.

On the other hand, we have known preteens with checking accounts. So, as you read this book, you will need to select and teach the parts that best fit the needs of your children.

No matter how old your children are, we suggest that you meet with them weekly for the first three months they are using our budgeting system. Perhaps you will have to meet with younger children even more frequently. These meetings will help them stay on the system until using it becomes a habit. Then, once they have learned the necessary skills, they will become independent in managing their money. We have learned from experience and from discussions with other parents and children that these budgeting meetings can be surprisingly productive and enjoyable.

The most important thing this book will do for you is to give you the confidence to be able to communicate effectively with your children about money. Our program will reduce your stress and increase your children's enjoyment, because they will know that if they want to spend money, they have the system, the skills, and the funds to be able to spend it. Also, when children are on a sound budget with an adequate allowance, their parents really spend less money on them because the children handle their own funds more effectively.

Just think how fortunate your children will be now and

as adults because they have learned to manage their money while they are young. Think also how fortunate you and your family will be.

At last, here is a proven budget system designed especially for young people—a comprehensive, but not complicated, system to teach them basic budgeting principles and procedures, a system to help them achieve and enjoy financial freedom for the rest of their lives.

To this end, and to the great young people of the world, we dedicate this book.

1

Earning, Spending, and Having Fun

You may be wondering, "How old should I be to read this book?" If you can read, and if you receive or earn money occasionally or regularly, you are old enough to become an expert at managing your money. That's what this book is all about.

How do you get your money? From an allowance or from gifts? From doing odd jobs, such as babysitting, washing the car, or mowing the lawn? Or from a regular part-time or full-time job? It doesn't matter where you get your money. In fact, it doesn't even matter how much money you make. What does matter is that you learn now how to handle your money properly. You might ask, "Why is it so important for me to learn this now, or even when I'm older?"

Think of it in this way: Suppose you had not learned to speak your native language by the time you first started school this year. You would have a hard time making friends and learning. It would take you a long time and a lot of hard work to learn a new language that late in life. You would really be angry when you realized you could have and should have learned it much sooner.

It is much the same with learning to handle your money. If you wait until you are an adult, you may already be in financial trouble. It will take time (maybe years) and hard work (maybe working two jobs) to get your financial affairs in order. If there was a system that could teach you how to avoid money problems for your whole life, wouldn't you want to learn it as soon as possible? Sure you would. And that system is in this book.

Think of something special you would like to buy or do. Now ask yourself, "Do I have the money to buy it or do it?" If you are like most people, your answer was probably no. Next, ask yourself, "If I keep earning and spending money as I am now, when will I be able to buy or do that special thing?" If your answer is bad news, don't worry—we have some good news for you.

As you read through this book, you will need to pick out the parts that apply to you. Do you keep your money in a small bank at home? Do you have a savings account? Do you have a checking account? Certain parts of this book talk about each of these things.

As you read this book, you will learn more if you work with your parents in learning to manage your money. We suggest that you meet with your parents at least once a week for ninety days to show them what you have learned and to get further suggestions from them. The younger you are, the more frequently you should meet with them. After the ninety days, you might meet with them once or twice a month. You should be able to learn the budget system described in this book very quickly. And once you have learned it, you'll be glad you did.

Now, let some young people who have already been on this budget system tell you about their success, fun, and happiness in learning to manage their money.

Natalie (age 16)

I'm a sophomore in high school, and I like to spend money. I work fifteen to twenty hours a week at the concession stand in a theater by our house. My family likes it because I can get them free passes to the movies. I like it because I make money!

I used to look at my paychecks and think of how much money I was making. But when I wanted to spend money, there never seemed to be any.

When my dad told me about the Financial Freedom Junior Budget System, I thought, "You've got to be kidding! Don't give me a budget. Give me money!"

But, anyway, I did learn to use the budget system, and it has really helped me. For the first time in my life I'm saving money, for lots of things, like college. I also have an emergency savings account for times when I need it. Since I have been on this system, I know where my money is and how much I have. I feel happy and responsible. And that's as much fun as spending money!

Devin (age 20)

I love my new car!

I can't say that the Financial Freedom Junior Budget System, paid for it, but I could never have bought a new car without it. By the end of last summer, I had been work-

ing for two months at a new job. Yet, I found myself worse off financially than when I took the job.

Then I learned about the Financial Freedom Junior Budget System. In the next two months, working only part-time, I was able to *double* my bank balance! And within five months, I ordered a brand new Honda Civic. Using the Financial Freedom Budget System, I got control of my money. And that put me behind the wheel of a new car!

Brent (age 22)

When I was fourteen, I never even thought about managing money. But I had always wanted a motorcycle, and after I learned to use the Financial Freedom Junior Budget System, I knew I could make my dream come true.

For two years, I budgeted and put a portion of the money I earned each month into a savings account. When I turned sixteen, I was able to pay cash for my motorcycle.

Learning to live on a budget was one of the best things I ever did. I've been able to buy and do the things I wanted. Now I'm in college. I'm going to use my budget to help pay my way through college and through life.

Sean (age 18)

I've been on a budget since I was eight. But when I started college, I told myself I was so smart that I didn't need to budget anymore. But it wasn't long until my spending was out of control. The odd thing was, I was working as a bill collector at the time, and I couldn't even control my own finances. One day, I went to the bank and found that I had plenty of money. The next day, my account was overdrawn. The only thing I could remember spending anything on was skiing, and that doesn't cost $700! About that time, I decided to start using the Financial Freedom Junior Budget System again.

After a few months, I found that my budget allowed me to do the things I enjoy (skiing and going to parties), pay my bills, and even have something left over.

I spend about an hour each month keeping my finances in order, but it's worth it. After all, I'd rather be skiing than talking to a bill collecter!

Kareina (age 11)

I started my budget at age six and have been using it for five years. My budget book has helped me a lot through

the last few years. I used to wonder how much money I had in the bank. Now I know exactly how much I have. Also, I know whether I can spend $80 at the mall or $50 on something else and not go bankrupt. That's why I love this budget system.

Slade (age 9)

Aren't you tired of asking your parents for money? Well, if you are, I've got just the thing for you—a budget! I know it sounds funny, but it helps you with your money. How? By showing you how much you have saved and how much you have left to spend. It's helped me buy things that I need. I've even gone to Denver with the money I've saved from my allowance.

If you save your money, your dreams will come true. If you don't spend any money till you're forty years old, you could buy your own limousine. But it would be hard to save that much money because it's too easy to spend money on toys or other things you want. Tell your parents about this. They'll get a kick out of it.

Kristen (age 15)

I think that a budget system is a good thing, especially when you're a teenager. I need money all the time for clothes and activities and other things. When I started working with my dad on budgeting, I thought it was stupid, but when I learned how much it helped me, I was glad. Now that I know how to do it, I really don't think about "budgeting," I just write everything down in my book. I'm happy because now I know exactly how much I have to spend, and I know how much I have saved up for things I will need in the long run—like a car! It's not hard to learn, and it really is helpful.

Shauna and Steve (married couple)

Some people learn about managing money the easy way—they study how to do it and then apply what they've learned. Not so with us. We learned the hard way, by making lots of mistakes.

When we were teenagers, we spent money without a care in the world. We weren't concerned about how to make money, and we didn't think about what would happen when the money ran out. We bought gifts for friends, bought lots of clothes, went out to eat all the time, and went to lots of movies. This kind of life was great, but then we got engaged.

All of a sudden, we realized that the money we earned would be our only source of income when we were married. We wouldn't be able to get money from our parents anymore.

Then Steve's father taught us how to set up a budget. Boy were we surprised to find out that our earnings were about $400 short of what we needed. We ended up changing our Hawaiian honeymoon to a honeymoon at Shauna's family's cabin.

For a while we were careful about our spending, but it seemed so hard. Finally, to get the things we wanted, we opened charge accounts and used them to their maximum limits. We bought things without worrying about how the monthly payments would affect us.

We kept on living that way until one day, bam! Our car broke down, and we were out of money. We had to humble ourselves, tell our parents what we had done, and ask for their help.

Our parents helped us out not only by lending us the money to fix the car, but by teaching us one more time how to budget our money. This time, the lesson sunk in.

Now, we don't buy as many "extras," but we don't have to worry about bill collectors calling or about not being able to buy groceries.

We both wish we had followed a budget as teenagers, because then we would have known how to manage our money when we got married. Also, we probably would have gone into marriage with big savings accounts!

2

Making Money

There are four main ways you can make money: (1) from an allowance, (2) from doing odd jobs around the house, (3) from doing odd jobs for other people, and (4) from part- or full-time employment. In this chapter, we will talk only about the first two—an allowance, and odd jobs around the house.

Receiving an Allowance

The word *allowance* means different things in different families. The most common meaning is a set amount of money you receive from your parents, usually monthly or weekly. An allowance is not pay for jobs. It is more like a gift. It comes with just being a member of the family. (This could mean you don't do any jobs at home. Or it could mean you do jobs but don't get paid for them. Or it could mean you may get paid for doing jobs separate from your allowance.)

In case you and your parents need help deciding how much of an allowance you should have, here are two possibilities:

1. One dollar a month for every year of your age. If

you are thirteen years old, you would get $13 a month. If you're sixteen, you would get $16 a month, and so on. Your parents may reduce your allowance when you get a part-time job, and they will probably stop it when you get a full-time job.

2. One dollar a month for every year of your school grade. A tenth-grader would get $10 a month. A twelfth-grader would get $12 a month.

These amounts may be more than your parents can afford to pay. If so, they might give you $.75 or $.50 a month for every year of your age.

Doing Odd Jobs

You may already do regular jobs around the house, yard, farm, or family business for pay. If not, maybe your parents would be willing to pay you to do some. Also, you might ask your parents to give you a job list. This is simply a list of odd jobs your parents would like you to do with the amount of money they are willing to pay you for each one. You and your parents might sit down together and make up such a list. Hang your list on the refrigerator, on the family bulletin board, in your room, or wherever you can see it easily.

Here are some examples of odd jobs. Ask your parents how much they might pay you to do them:

Washing and waxing the kitchen floor
Vacuuming the family room
Washing the car
Dusting the furniture
Mowing the lawn
Weeding the garden
Babysitting

Polishing the furniture
Taking out the garbage
Cleaning the tools
Sweeping the garage
Sweeping the sidewalks
Doing the dishes (other than your assigned day)
Cleaning the bathroom
Ironing the clothes
Trimming the yard
Making a meal
Cleaning the bird cage
Bathing the dog
Washing windows

You can probably think of many more to add to the list. These jobs might run for a week, a month, or any length of time that you and your parents agree upon.

In some families, there is another kind of household job, called "chores." Chores are the jobs you are expected to do without being paid so you can feel like a contributing member of your family. Examples of such chores may be making your bed, cleaning your own room, vacuuming the floor, and so on.

Even though there are many things in your family that you ought to do without pay, we believe that you should receive an allowance, even if it is very small, but not for doing jobs. Also, when possible, you should earn money by doing some odd jobs around the house. Having your own money is the first step in learning to manage it well.

3

Banking Your Money

Where should you keep the money you make? There are two places—the "home bank" and the "away-from-home bank."

Home Bank

Most likely, you already have some kind of bank at home. It may be a piggy bank or some other kind of store-bought bank shaped like a car, a cartoon character, or an animal. It may be a cookie jar, a small safe, a jewelry box, or maybe just a cardboard box, a tin can, or a bottle. It doesn't make any difference what you use, as long as you have some kind of bank at home so your money doesn't lie around loose. If you don't have a home bank, find one that you can use.

After you have your home bank, keep your money in it. Put the bank in your room. You may consider keeping it out of sight, or even hiding it, for safekeeping. But be sure you always know where it is and how much money is in it.

Away-from-Home Bank

We recommend that everyone, at the earliest age possible, have a savings account at a bank away from home.

Maybe your parents opened a savings account for you before you were old enough to do it yourself, or maybe you have already opened one yourself. If you already have a savings account, we congratulate you. If you don't have a savings account, and you think you have enough money to open one, we will explain how to do it.

There are four kinds of financial institutions in which you may open a savings account:

1. Banks
2. Savings and loans institutions
3. Industrial loan and finance companies
4. Credit unions

There isn't much difference between these four institutions when it comes to savings accounts, and in this book we will refer to them all as "banks."

We recommend that you call or visit at least one bank in your area to learn what you need to do to open your savings account.

Some banks require you to deposit a certain amount of money to open your savings account. This is called the "minimum deposit." Most banks require that you have your own Social Security number before you can open a savings account. Some banks will also require, if you are under the age of eighteen, that your parents sign with you on the account. If so, you will need their approval before you can withdraw any money.

You may already know that banks will pay you for depositing your money in a savings account. The money they pay is called "interest." The more money you have in your savings account and the longer you leave it there, the more money the bank will pay you. How much money they will pay is a certain percentage (set by the bank) of the amount of money you have in your savings account.

When they pay you this money, they usually just add it to your savings. The wonderful thing about this is that then you can earn interest on that money, too. This is called "compound interest." If you don't withdraw the interest you earn, it will continue to earn more. This can add up to quite a lot of savings over a few years.

The higher the interest rate the bank pays, the more money you will make. Let's say that you have $50 to deposit in your savings account. One bank may pay you 4 percent interest (or $2.00 a year) on your $50. But another bank may pay you 5 percent interest (or $2.50 a year). Which bank would you choose? The one that pays 5 percent, of course.

When you are looking for a bank for your savings account, you may want to find out what other services the bank has. For instance, someday you will want a checking account, a credit card, and opportunities to borrow money when you need it. You might want to ask about safe deposit boxes, where you can keep valuable things besides money.

There are different types of savings accounts. Let's take a look at the three most common:

1. *The passbook account.* If you have this kind of account, the bank will give you a little book called a "passbook." Whenever you put money into your account or take money out of it, someone at the bank will record in your book how much you deposited or how much you withdrew. Some banks will not give you a passbook. Instead they will send you a statement once every three months that tells you what your deposits and withdrawals were during those three months. This account pays a certain amount of interest annually, and you can make deposits and withdrawals whenever you like. Most of the

time, there is a minimum amount of money that you have to deposit to open the account. This could be as low as $25, but it will vary from bank to bank. Usually, you must leave a certain amount of your money in your savings account as a "minimum balance." If you don't, the bank might close your account. This minimum amount is usually somewhere between $25 and $50.

2. The second type of savings account is called a *money market account*. This type of account pays a higher rate of interest, and it pays part of it every day. Usually you can make deposits and withdrawals whenever you want, but the banks require a much higher amount of money to open the account, and you must also maintain a certain minimum balance. Some banks require a minimum amount of $1,000, and some may require as much as $2,500. If the balance dips below the required amount, some banks charge a service charge of $5 or $10 per month. Also, you wouldn't get as high an interest rate for those days until you put the minimum amount back in your account. Unless you can keep a lot of money in the bank all the time, a money market account is not for you.

3. The third type of savings account is called a *time certificate of deposit,* often called a "CD." CD's pay higher rates of interest than passbook accounts, but with a CD, you must leave your money in the bank for a certain time, such as 30 days, 90 days, 180 days, 1 year, 2 years, or 3 years. Banks usually require you to deposit a certain amount in a CD, depending on how long the CD is for. For instance, one bank may require a minimum amount of $500 if the CD is for over one year and $1,000 if it is less than one year. The interest rate is based on how long you have to leave your money in the CD. Generally, the longer the time, the higher the interest rate you will get. How-

ever, you won't be able to withdraw from a CD before the time is up.

We recommend that your first account be with a bank near your home, and that it be a passbook savings account.

If you don't have enough money right now to open your savings account, you will want to consider all the ways possible for you to earn some money so you can do it as soon as possible.

If you already have money at home, you need to decide how much of it you want to deposit in your savings account. We recommend that you keep some money at home so you won't have to go to the bank every time you want to buy something. You should keep about as much money as you plan to spend during the coming month. If you keep more than that at home, you are cheating yourself out of interest you could be earning. Also, your money could get lost or stolen, so the less you have around the house, the less you could lose. A third reason to not have too much money around is because of the tremendous temptation to spend it on unplanned things. When it is tucked away in your savings account, it is not only safer from being lost, but safer from being misspent.

Once you have enough money, take your savings (and your parents, if necessary) and head for the bank. Every bank is eager to have you for a customer, so they will be very friendly and helpful to you. Don't think because you are young or because you are not going to deposit a lot of money to start with, that they will not be interested in you. They like people who start savings accounts while they are young because they hope to keep them as a customer for many years to come.

When you talk to the banker, you can ask all the questions you want. After your questions have been answered, the banker will ask you some, and you will need to write down the answers on one or more forms. You will need to give the bank your name, address, phone number, Social Security number, and things like that.

Next, the banker will take your money and give you a passbook or a receipt. Keep your passbook in a safe place. If the bank doesn't give you a passbook, they will mail you a monthly statement that will tell you the same information as if you had a passbook.

4

Planning to Spend

Next to actually spending your money, the most fun thing is to plan how you want to spend it. The main reason to plan ahead of time how you want to spend your money is so you will already have your mind made up when the chance to spend it comes along. Many people don't plan what they want to spend their money on, so they buy things they later wished they hadn't. Unplanned spending is called "impulse spending."

Impulse spending can be as simple as when you go out for a hamburger and a drink, the clerk asks you if you want french fries, and you say yes. Or, you go to buy a pair of jogging shoes and end up buying two pairs because the clerk suggests that you may want a different pair for tennis. In both cases, you didn't really plan on spending as much as you did. That means you won't have money later for things you want more or need worse.

Planning what you want to spend your money on is called "budgeting." Your spending plan is your budget.

How to Plan Your Budget

Take a blank piece of paper and write "Budget Categories" on the left side at the top. (Budget categories

19

are the things you will spend your money on.) Write the numbers 1 through 20 down the left side of the paper under the words "Budget Categories." This will give you up to twenty different items (budget categories) you can plan to spend your money on. (We call this the "scratch-paper" method of budgeting.)

At the top of your paper, in the middle, write the words "Budget Amounts." The budget amounts are the amounts of money you decide to spend on the budget categories.

Write "Money Available" on the right side of the paper, also at the top. "Money available" means how much money you have right now to start your budget. Underneath "Money Available," write the amount of money you have available right now.

Budget Categories	Budget Amounts	Money Available
1.		
2.		
3.		
4.		
5.		
6.		
7.		
8.		
9.		
10.		
11.		
12.		
13.		
14.		
15.		
16.		
17.		
18.		
19.		
20.		

Now you are ready to decide how you want to spend your money. Think of all the things you spend it on now and the things you would like to spend it on in the future. To save you some time, we have listed thirty of the most common things (budget categories) that young people spend their money on:

Cleaning/Laundry	Entertainment
Clothing	Savings
Contributions	School Supplies
Debt Payments	Self-Improvement
Food (at restaurants)	Subscriptions
Gifts	Telephone
Groceries (at home)	Toys
Hobbies	Treats
Housing	Tuition
Insurance	Utilities
Investments	Vacation/Trip
Medical/Dental	Vehicles—Gas
Miscellaneous	Vehicles—Loan
Petty Cash	Vehicles—Other

As you choose each budget category you want to use, write it on your paper under the words "Budget Categories." The average young person has about eight budget categories. If you have fewer or more than that, it's all right—this is *your* budget.

To show you how a budget works, we will use four budget categories: Savings, Clothes, Entertainment, and Gifts. We will say you have $50 in your "Money Available" column. Your budget would now look like this:

Budget Categories	Budget Amounts	Money Available
		$50.00
1. Savings		
2. Clothes		
3. Entertainment		
4. Gifts		

You then decide how much of your money (from your "Money Available") you want to spend on each of the budget categories you chose. Let us say you budget $10 for savings. You write $10 under "Budget Amounts" across from "Savings." To find out how much money you have left, you write $10 under the $50 in the "Money Available" column. Then, you subtract that $10 from the $50, giving you $40 left to budget (spend):

Budget Categories	Budget Amounts	Money Available
		$50.00
1. Savings	$10.00	−10.00
		40.00
2. Clothes		
3. Entertainment		
4. Gifts		

Continuing, you decide to budget $20 for "Clothing." You write that amount under "Budget Amounts" next to "Clothing." You subtract that $20 from the $40 you had left under "Money Available," leaving $20 more to budget. Next, you decide to budget $15 for "Entertainment." You write that $15 on the same line as "Entertainment." Then you subtract it from the remaining $20, which gives you $5 left to budget. That last $5 is budgeted to "Gifts," and you are now finished budgeting your money. Your budget would now look like this:

Budget Categories	Budget Amounts	Money Available
		$50.00
1. Savings	$10.00	−10.00
		40.00
2. Clothes	20.00	−20.00
		20.00
3. Entertainment	15.00	−15.00
		5.00
4. Gifts	5.00	−5.00
		.00

Remember, you should write on your paper your own budget categories and budget amounts, not the ones in the example.

The Budget Builder

If you would like to plan your budget in a little more detail, you can use the Budget Builder form on the next page. This form will help you see, on one piece of paper, (a) where your money comes from, (b) how much money you get from each of those sources, (c) all the places you keep it, (d) how much money you have right now, (e) the different things you want to spend your money on, and (f) how much money you want to spend on each one of those things.

Budget Builder

A. Income Sources	B. Income per Month	C. Savings Places	D. Money Available	E. Budget Categories	F. Budget Amounts
_____	_____	_____	_____	_____	_____
_____	_____	_____	_____	_____	_____
_____	_____	_____	_____	_____	_____
_____	_____	_____	_____	_____	_____
_____	_____	_____	_____	_____	_____
_____	_____	_____	_____	_____	_____
_____	_____	_____	_____	_____	_____
Total $_____		Total $_____		_____	_____
				_____	_____
				_____	_____
				_____	_____
				_____	_____
				_____	_____
				_____	_____
				_____	_____
				_____	_____
				_____	_____
				_____	_____
				_____	_____
				Total	$ _____

To use the form, follow these instructions:

1. Write in column A all the different ways you receive money. Examples are allowance, gifts, interest on your savings, odd jobs, and regular part-time or full-time employment.

2. Write in column B how much money you receive every month from each of those sources. If you don't make the same amount of money each month, just write down about how much you usually receive. Add up all the money you make and write the amount on the line labeled "total" under B.

3. Write in column C all the different places you keep your money. Examples are "home" bank, savings accounts, checking account, your secret "stash of cash," your pocket, and so on.

4. Write in column D how much money you have in each of those places right now. Add up the money you have listed in column D and write the amount on the line labeled "Total" under the column.

5. Write in column E all the ways you plan to spend your money. These are your budget categories.

6. Write in column F the amount of money you plan to spend for each of your budget categories. The money you will budget for each of your budget categories comes from the money you wrote down in column D. In other words, if you don't have it, you don't budget it. You can use the blank space on the left side of the form to do your figuring.

Add up your figures in column F and write total in the space provided under the column. Your total should equal the amount on the "Total" line under column D. Now your budget is finished.

Budgeting by Percentage

Rather than deciding on specific *amounts* to spend on your budget categories, you may want to decide what *percentage* of your money you will spend on them. Then if the amount of money you make changes, you can easily figure out the change for every category without making up entirely new amounts.

To budget by percentage, write under Budget Amounts the percent of the total "Money Available" you want to budget to each of your budget categories. Then figure the dollar amount of each percentage and write in the actual amounts next to the percentages. You can budget by percentage using either a sheet of paper or the Budget Builder.

Suppose you have $50 under "Money Available" in column D of the Budget Builder. You decide to spend 20 percent of that $50 on savings. You write 20% under "Budget Amounts" in column F on the left side of the line next to "Savings." Next, in the scratch-pad space on the form, you subtract 20% from 100%, which leaves 80% to budget.

Next, you decide to spend 40 percent of your money for clothing. You write that percentage on the left side of the line under "Budget Amounts" in column F across from the word "Clothing" under "Budget Categories" in column E. You subtract 40% from the remaining 80%, which leaves 40% to budget.

Next, you budget 30% to "Entertainment" and write it in column F. You subtract 30% from 40%, in the scratch-pad space, which leaves a balance to budget of 10%.

Finally, you budget the remaining 10% to "Gifts" and also write that under "Budget Amounts" in column F on the left side of the line.

Now, you go back to the top of "Budget Amounts" in column F and multiply the percentage on each line by the total amount of money under "Money Available" in column D. This will give you actual dollar figures for each budget category.

For example, you multiply your total $50 under "Money Available" by .20 (20%) for "Savings," which gives you $10. You write the $10 to the right of the 20% on the same line under "Budget Amounts" in column F. Then, you multiply $50 total by .40 (40%) for "Clothing," which gives you $20. You write $20 to the right of the 40% on the same line under "Budget Amounts." Next, you multiply your $50 by .30 (30%) for "Entertainment," which gives you $15. You write that figure under "Budget Amounts." Finally, you multiply the $50 by .10 (10%) for "Gifts," which gives you $5. You write that in the same column.

To check your math, add up the figures under "Budget Amounts." The total should be the same as the total under "Money Available" (in this example, $50). If it is not, re-check your figures and make the necessary corrections. Your budget is now complete. Your Budget Builder should look like the one on the next page.

Budget Builder

A. Income Sources	B. Income per Month	C. Savings Places	D. Money Available	E. Budget Categories	F. Budget Amounts
Work for John			$50.00	Savings	20% $10.00
				Clothing	40% $20.00
				Entertain	30% $15.00
				Gifts	10% $5.00
Total $ _____		Total $ 50.00			

Scratch Pad Space

Savings
$50.00
x .20
$10.00

Clothing	100%
$50.00	−20%
x .40	80%
$20.00	−40%
Entertain.	40%
$50.00	−30%
x .30	10%
$15.00	−10%
	0

Gifts
$50.00
x .10
$5.00

Total $ 50.00

5

The Financial Freedom
Junior Budget Booklet

If you wanted to sew up an unstitched seam, you would want to use the best tool possible—a needle. If you wanted to tighten a screw, again, you would want to use the best tool possible—a screwdriver. It makes just as much sense that to manage your money in the best way possible, you would want the best tool possible—The Financial Freedom Junior Budget Booklet! The booklet looks like this, and you will find an actual budget booklet in the back of this book.

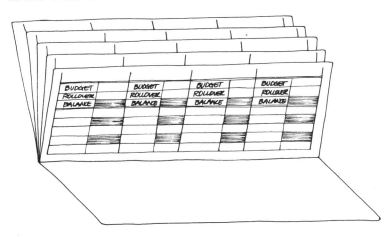

The booklet is little, but it will make a big difference in your financial success. Because it is small, it is easy to use, easy to store, and easy to carry with you.

It is also the fastest budget system we know of. It takes an average of seven seconds to record each spending transaction. That means if you spend money 100 times in a month, you will take only 12 minutes a month to keep track of what you have spent.

The average young person will use one budget booklet a month. If you have very few deposits and don't spend money many times during a month, one booklet may last you two or even three months. Of course, if you have many deposits and expenses during a month, you might use more than one booklet a month.

Inside the front cover of the budget booklet are instructions on how to order more of the booklets. The ones you order will come assembled and in a box of twelve.

On the back of the booklet are spaces where you can write your budget categories and amounts.

CATEGORY	FIRST PAYCHECK	SECOND PAYCHECK	CATEGORY	FIRST PAYCHECK	SECOND PAYCHECK
1.			11.		
2.			12.		
3.			13.		
4.			14.		
5.			15.		
6.			16.		
7.			17.		
8.			18.		
9.			19.		
10.			20.		

NAME _____ MONTH _____ YEAR _____   TOTAL _____ _____

Inside the booklet are five pages, and each page has four columns. This gives you spaces in which to write up to twenty spending categories. You write your spending categories in the white space at the top of as many columns as you need. Under the categories, next to the word "Budget," you write the amount of money (or the percent) you have budgeted for each category. By the word "Rollover," you write the amount of money you have left over (or are short) from your past booklet in each category.

Then, next to the word "Balance," in the shaded area, you write the beginning balance for each category. If this is your first month, then your balance will be the amount of your money you budgeted for that spending category. From the second month on, you will add the rollover amounts to (or subtract them from) your budgeted amounts to get your balances.

June

Savings		Clothing		Entertainment		Gifts	
BUDGET	10.00	BUDGET	20.00	BUDGET	15.00	BUDGET	5.00
ROLLOVER	—	ROLLOVER	—	ROLLOVER	—	ROLLOVER	—
BALANCE	10.00	BALANCE	20.00	BALANCE	15.00	BALANCE	5.00
Date / Check #		Date / Check #		Date / Check #		Date / Check #	
For / From		For / From		For / From		For / From	
Date / Check #		Date / Check #		Date / Check #		Date / Check #	
For / From		For / From		For / From		For / From	
Date / Check #		Date / Check #		Date / Check #		Date / Check #	
For / From		For / From		For / From		For / From	
Date / Check #		Date / Check #		Date / Check #		Date / Check #	
For / From		For / From		For / From		For / From	
Date / Check #		Date / Check #		Date / Check #		Date / Check #	
For / From		For / From		For / From		For / From	

There is a space to write the date every time you spend or deposit money. It's just to the left of where you write the dollar amount. Also, just below that, is a space to write what you spent your money for, which is shortened simply to "For."

Spending from Your Home Bank

Suppose you want to go to a movie with your friends. You decide you want to take $5. Go to your booklet, which should be right next to your home bank. Find the spending category that says "Fun" or "Entertainment." You see that you have a $15 balance in that category. Write in your booklet, in the top half of the box space marked "Date/Check #", the date you are taking the money out of your home bank. Then write "movie" in the bottom half of the box space marked "For/From." Subtract $5 from your $15 and write the new balance of $10 in the shaded area to the right of "For/From." This lets you know what is left to spend in that category. (Be sure you place a minus sign by the $5 to show that you subtracted it from your bank.) Finally, get out your bank and take out the $5.

June

Savings		Clothing		Entertainment		Gifts	
BUDGET	10.00	BUDGET	20.00	BUDGET	15.00	BUDGET	5.00
ROLLOVER	—	ROLLOVER	—	ROLLOVER	—	ROLLOVER	—
BALANCE	10.00	BALANCE	20.00	BALANCE	15.00	BALANCE	5.00
Date / Check #		Date / Check #		Date / Check # June 3	-5.00	Date / Check #	
For / From		For / From		For / From Movie	10.00	For / From	
Date / Check #		Date / Check #		Date / Check #		Date / Check #	
For / From		For / From		For / From		For / From	
Date / Check #		Date / Check #		Date / Check #		Date / Check #	
For / From		For / From		For / From		For / From	
Date / Check #		Date / Check #		Date / Check #		Date / Check #	
For / From		For / From		For / From		For / From	
Date / Check #		Date / Check #		Date / Check #		Date / Check #	
For / From		For / From		For / From		For / From	

One of the main benefits of this system is that after you spend some money, you know exactly how much you have left to spend next time. So, before you take off for the movie, you know that you have $10 left in this spending category.

Let's try another example. Suppose you decide to buy a birthday gift for a friend. You look in your budget booklet under the "Gifts" category, and you see that you have $5 left to spend. Because this person is such a good friend, you decide to spend all of the $5 on the gift.

In your booklet, in the "Date/Check" space, you write the date you are taking the money out of your bank. Then, in the "For/From" space, you write your friend's name. Then you subtract the $5 that you are going to spend from the $5 in the "Gifts" category, giving you a new balance of $0. Now you're ready to go shopping. In addition, you are managing wisely the money in your home bank.

June

Savings		Clothing		Entertainment		Gifts	
BUDGET	10.00	BUDGET	20.00	BUDGET	15.00	BUDGET	5.00
ROLLOVER	—	ROLLOVER	—	ROLLOVER	—	ROLLOVER	—
BALANCE	10.00	BALANCE	20.00	BALANCE	15.00	BALANCE	5.00
Date / Check #		Date / Check #		Date / Check # June 3	-5.00	Date / Check # June 11	-5.00
For / From		For / From		For / From Movie	10.00	For / From Chris	.00
Date / Check #		Date / Check #		Date / Check #		Date / Check #	
For / From		For / From		For / From		For / From	
Date / Check #		Date / Check #		Date / Check #		Date / Check #	
For / From		For / From		For / From		For / From	
Date / Check #		Date / Check #		Date / Check #		Date / Check #	
For / From		For / From		For / From		For / From	
Date / Check #		Date / Check #		Date / Check #		Date / Check #	
For / From		For / From		For / From		For / From	

Spending from Your Savings Account

Suppose you have decided to go shopping for clothes. We recommend you go to at least two different stores to compare items and prices. Or, you might read some newspaper ads before you leave home and find the store that has what you want for the price you want to pay. The next thing you need to do is check your booklet to see how much money you have in your "Clothing" category. Thanks to your good planning, saving, and shopping research, you have enough.

You head for the bank with your passbook and your booklet. At the bank, you fill out a withdrawal slip, which has places for you to write your name, your account number, the date, and the amount of money that you wish to withdraw. Then you sign it and give it to the bank teller. The teller takes your passbook and withdrawal slip, and gives you the money you asked for. (By the way, you can do all this by mail if you want to.)

When you receive the money—let's say $20—from your clothing budget, in the top half of the space under "Clothing," write the date that you withdrew the money from your passbook savings account in the "Date/Check Number" space. In the bottom part of the space, "For/ From," write what you will spend your money on. In this case, it would be clothes. You may want to write the name of the store where you will buy your clothes.

The final step is to write -$20 in the space, bringing down the new balance of $0. Now you are ready to buy whatever you planned.

Suppose you want to spend $40 for clothes in a certain month, but you have only $20 in your booklet.

June

Savings		Clothing		Entertainment		Gifts	
BUDGET	10.00	BUDGET	20.00	BUDGET	15.00	BUDGET	5.00
ROLLOVER	—	ROLLOVER	—	ROLLOVER	—	ROLLOVER	—
BALANCE	10.00	BALANCE	20.00	BALANCE	15.00	BALANCE	5.00
Date / Check #		Date / Check # June 15	-20.00	Date / Check # June 3	-5.00	Date / Check # June 11	-5.00
For / From		For / From Pants	.00	For / From Movie	10.00	For / From Chris	.00
Date / Check #		Date / Check #		Date / Check #		Date / Check #	
For / From		For / From		For / From		For / From	
Date / Check #		Date / Check #		Date / Check #		Date / Check #	
For / From		For / From		For / From		For / From	
Date / Check #		Date / Check #		Date / Check #		Date / Check #	
For / From		For / From		For / From		For / From	
Date / Check #		Date / Check #		Date / Check #		Date / Check #	
For / From		For / From		For / From		For / From	

You would save your money until the following month and add it to your new $20 clothing budget. That will give you the $40 you need.

Depositing Money

Now you need to know how to deposit money into your bank at home and your savings account using your booklet. Let's say you just earned $10 for doing a job for a neighbor. If you will be spending it within the month, then you will probably put it in your bank at home. If not, take your $10, your passbook, and your booklet to make a deposit in your savings account. At the bank, you will fill out a deposit slip, which requires about the same information as a withdrawal slip. The teller will give you a receipt if you have a statement savings account or make an entry in your passbook showing the $10 deposit in your account.

After you have made your deposit, you decide how to budget the $10. Let's say you decide to save half of your

$10. Under the savings category, you write the date of the deposit and the amount of $5. Then, in the "For/From" space, you write where the money came from. You add $5 to the $10 already there, which gives you $15 in savings.

This leaves you $5 left to budget. Let's say that you decide to spend the $5 on clothes. Under the "Clothing" category, you again write the date of the deposit and the amount of $5. In the "For/From" space, you again write where the money came from. Finally, you bring down the new balance, which is $5. Now you have finished making and recording your deposit.

June

Savings		Clothing		Entertainment		Gifts	
BUDGET	10.00	BUDGET	20.00	BUDGET	15.00	BUDGET	5.00
ROLLOVER	—	ROLLOVER	—	ROLLOVER	—	ROLLOVER	—
BALANCE	10.00	BALANCE	20.00	BALANCE	15.00	BALANCE	5.00
Date / Check # June 18	+5.00	Date / Check # June 15	−20.00	Date / Check # June 3	−5.00	Date / Check # June 11	−5.00
For / From work for John	15.00	For / From Pants	.00	For / From Movie	10.00	For / From Chris	.00
Date / Check #		Date / Check # June 18	+5.00	Date / Check #		Date / Check #	
For / From		For / From work for John	5.00	For / From		For / From	
Date / Check #		Date / Check #		Date / Check #		Date / Check #	
For / From		For / From		For / From		For / From	
Date / Check #		Date / Check #		Date / Check #		Date / Check #	
For / From		For / From		For / From		For / From	
Date / Check #		Date / Check #		Date / Check #		Date / Check #	
For / From		For / From		For / From		For / From	

What if you have taken $20 out of your bank or savings account but you spend only $15, leaving you with $5 that you didn't spend?

There are two things you can do with the $5. (1) You can spend it on anything you want, maybe as a bonus for living within your budget, or (2) you redeposit the $5 into your home bank or savings account and then write the deposit as usual in your budget booklet. We feel that it is best to redeposit the money so that the next time that you want to spend from that category, instead of having a zero balance, you will have some additional money to spend that you weren't counting on. Because you followed the principles of budgeting, you will have money for another time that you would really like to buy something.

The Rollover

Let us say, at this point, that a new month is starting and that you have decided to use a new budget booklet for the new month. In your old booklet, you still have some money in some of the categories. For example, you have $15 in savings, $5 in your clothing category, and $10 in your entertainment category. You will need to "roll over" these amounts into your new budget booklet.

To do this, you prepare your new budget booklet for the new month. You write in the categories—"Savings," "Clothes," "Entertainment," and "Gifts"—at the very top of the budget booklet. The next space is labeled "Budget." In this space, you record your budget amounts for the new month. Let's suppose that you have not yet received any money this month. In that case, you would put $0 under the four categories. Or, if you use the percentage method, you would write in the percent you will spend in each category, when you do receive some money during the month.

The next space is labeled "Rollover." In this space you write the balances left over in the categories from your other booklet. Under "Savings," you would write $15, under "Clothes," $5, under "Entertainment," $10, and under "Gifts," $0.

The next space is labeled "Balance." To get your beginning balance, you would add your budgeted amounts to your rollover. Under "Savings," you would have $0 as the budgeted amount plus $15 in rollover. This gives you a beginning balance of $15. In "Clothing," you would have $0 for the budgeted amount, $5 for the rollover, and a new beginning balance of $5. Under "Entertainment," you would have $0 as the budgeted amount, $10 as the rollover, and a new beginning balance of $10. Finally under "Gifts," you would have a $0 budgeted amount (because you spent it in the previous examples) plus $0 as rollover, so your new beginning balance would be $0. When you are done, you will be ready to begin spending for the new month, and your new budget booklet will look something like this.

July

Savings		Clothing		Entertainment		Gifts	
BUDGET	.00	BUDGET	.00	BUDGET	.00	BUDGET	.00
ROLLOVER	15.00	ROLLOVER	5.00	ROLLOVER	10.00	ROLLOVER	.00
BALANCE	15.00	BALANCE	5.00	BALANCE	10.00	BALANCE	.00
Date / Check #		Date / Check #		Date / Check #		Date / Check #	
For / From		For / From		For / From		For / From	
Date / Check #		Date / Check #		Date / Check #		Date / Check #	
For / From		For / From		For / From		For / From	
Date / Check #		Date / Check #		Date / Check #		Date / Check #	
For / From		For / From		For / From		For / From	
Date / Check #		Date / Check #		Date / Check #		Date / Check #	
For / From		For / From		For / From		For / From	
Date / Check #		Date / Check #		Date / Check #		Date / Check #	
For / From		For / From		For / From		For / From	

You may be wondering how you can get more money to put into your various budget categories. You can do this by working hard on the job list you have made with your parents, by saving your allowance, or by doing odd jobs for neighbors and friends. Remember, you can have anything you want financially as long as you plan for it with enough time and work.

6

Saving Your Money

After you use the budget booklet for a few months, you will find that you are spending less and enjoying it more. You will enjoy it more because you will be saving for the things you really want.

Most people don't save very much money. And most who do save, don't do it very consistently. Most people who have a savings account use it as a "put" and "take" account. That is, they put their money in and then almost immediately take it out again. If you are wise, you will regularly put money into your savings account and keep it there for a while so it will earn interest to buy more of what you want.

We recommend that you save 10 percent of all the money you earn every single month. If you do this while you are young, the chances are very high that you will do it for the rest of your life. And saving money is one of the main ways you will get more of what you want in life.

However, right now, you may be thinking, "Since I'm just starting this plan, I really can't save that much." Maybe so. Start by saving 1 percent, or 3 percent, or 5 percent—whatever you can save at first. But save something each month, no matter how small the amount. Set your goal to gradually build up to saving 10 percent of your earnings.

Also, we recommend that you budget your savings into three general savings categories, just as you budgeted your spending into several spending categories. The three general savings categories we suggest are: (1) short term, (2) long term, and (3) emergency.

Savings Categories

Short-term savings are for the things you want to buy or do in the next year or two. For example, one girl wanted to make the high-school swim team the next year of school, so she saved for a year so she could attend a summer swimming camp. A fourteen-year-old boy began saving for the down payment on a small 4x4 truck to buy when he became sixteen.

Long-term savings are for things you want to buy or do a few years in the future. For example, one fifteen-year-old girl began saving for a trip to London she planned to take after her graduation from high school. One thirteen-year-old girl started saving to go away to college. And one eighteen-year-old young man set a goal to save enough money for a down payment on a house by the time he would be 25.

Emergency savings are for unplanned expenses, such as replacing a bike that is wrecked by a hit-and-run driver. One young man went to work one summer in Hawaii and didn't find out until he got there that he had to pay $75 for special work clothes. Another use for emergency savings is when you want or need to spend more money one month than you have in one of your spending categories.

Budgeting Your Savings

Just as you budgeted your money for spending, you should also budget your money for your savings.

The first method of budgeting your savings is to decide how much of your savings will go into each of the three savings categories each month. One month you may put more in one category than the others because you spent money out of it and you need to build it back up. You should always try to put some money into each of the three categories every month.

The second method of budgeting your savings is the percentage method. You decide what percentage of what you save each month will go into your three savings categories. That way you do not have to redecide every month the actual dollar figure to put in each one. This helps keep you well-rounded in your savings because you are not tempted to put too much into one category and too little into another.

We suggest that you start by budgeting 50 percent to short-term savings, 30 percent to long-term savings, and 20 percent to emergency savings. These amounts are merely guidelines, but you should save something in each category every month.

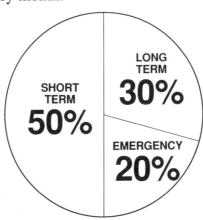

Recording Your Savings

There are three ways to record your savings in your budget booklet.

The first method, which we favor, is the three-column method. You use three columns in your budget booklet. Label one "Short-term," one "Long-Term," and one "Emergency." Next to each of these categories, write the percentage of your savings that will go into it when you make a deposit.

The second method is to decide, in dollars, how much of your savings will go to each category.

The third recording method is the one-column method. You simply use the word "savings" in your budget booklet as one of your budgeting categories. All the money you save each month, plus all the money already in your savings account, would be shown there.

You may want to break down your savings categories into specific things you are saving for. If you use this fourth method, you can just use one or more of your unused columns in your budget booklet.

Answers to Frequent Questions

People sometimes ask, "Suppose I receive $20 as a gift. What do you recommend I do with it?" Our recommendation is to put it into one or more of your three savings categories.

Another question often asked is, "Do I need three separate savings accounts for those three savings categories?" No, because you keep track of how much money you have in those three savings categories in your budget booklet, so it doesn't matter that it is all mixed together in your savings account.

7

The Checking Account

If you know you are ready for a checking account, or if you want to find out if you are ready for one, you should read this chapter. If you already have one, you may still find this chapter helpful.

Paying with checks rather than cash has become the most popular way to buy things in the world today. The question is probably not *if* you will have a checking account, but *when*. You should consider two major points before opening a checking account.

1. *Your age*. As a general rule, we do not recommend opening a checking account before age sixteen. Normally, a young person would open a checking account at age eighteen or just after high-school graduation. For those under eighteen, most banks require that a parent co-sign on the account to guarantee that if the young person writes checks for more money than there is in the account, the parents will pay the shortage or "overdraft."

2. *Your income and expenses*. When your income is quite stable, from part or full-time employment (not just odd jobs), then you are closer to needing a checking account. Usually, as your income increases, so does your

spending. Going back and forth for frequent deposits and withdrawals in your savings account becomes a real bother. With a checking account, instead of your going to the bank, the bank comes to you. Keeping a lot of cash around the house or carrying it with you becomes a big security risk. Having your checkbook stolen or lost is not usually as serious as having cash stolen or lost.

Before you open your checking account, we recommend that you call two or more financial institutions that offer checking accounts. Try banks, savings and loan companies, and credit unions. Be sure to check the bank where you already have your savings account.

Some of the information you will want to find out is: (1) the types of checking accounts available, (2) the minimum amount needed to open an account, (3) the minimum age requirement, (4) co-signing requirements, (5) service charges, (6) check protection, (7) availability of a bank card (different from a credit card), (8) overdraft charges, and (9) cost of checks.

A bank card looks very much like a credit card, but it is used like a check. When you pay for something with a credit card, your account is not charged with that expense for about thirty days. But when you pay for something with a bank card, your checking account is charged with that expense as soon as it reaches the bank—just like a check. The bank card is becoming more popular for two reasons. First, it saves you the effort of writing a check because the store clerk fills out a form for you to sign. However, you still fill out your check register and budget booklet with the same information as you would if you had written a check. Second, it is being accepted by more and more merchants all the time as a substitute for a check.

A checking account has two main parts: (1) the checks themselves, and (2) the check register, where you will record your spending and deposits.

The Check

The first part of a checking account is the checks themselves. When you open your checking account, you will get to decide how many checks you want to order and what design you want on them, if any. Designed checks will cost you more than plain ones. Some banks offer plain checks at no charge. You will usually order one box to start off with and see how long those last you.

You may order checks with your name, address, and phone number pre-printed on each check. Many businesses will not accept a check that does not have that pre-printed information on it.

A typical check looks like this:

```
┌───────────────────────────────────────────────────────┐
│                                               0000      │
│              JOHN DOE JR.                               │
│            1234 Neighbor Lane                           │
│            Anytown, USA  99999                          │
│               222-0000              _____19____      │
│                                                         │
│   Pay  to the                                           │
│   order of _____  $ _____  │
│                                                         │
│   _____ Dollars       │
│                                                         │
│                                                         │
│   For _____    _____         │
│                                                         │
└───────────────────────────────────────────────────────┘
```

Notice that there are lines for you to write in the date and year. Also, there is a space to write the name of the person you are paying. This space is labeled "Pay to the order of." There are two places to write the amount of money the check is for, one in numbers and one in letters. This helps avoid confusion over the check amount if you should not write it clearly or if it gets smudged. On the bottom left-hand corner is a line where you can write what the check paid for.

Finally, there is a space at the bottom where you sign your name. Your signature tells the bank that they have your permission to take that much money out of your checking account and pay it to the person cashing it.

Here is a check that has been filled out: The check is from Jane Doe, check #10, dated May 17, 1987, payable to "Any Store," in the amount of $20 (written once in numbers and once in letters), for shoes (on sale) for Mom's gift. And, Jane signed it.

JANE DOE		0010
1234 Neighbor Lane		
Anytown, USA 99999		
222-0000	_May 17_ 19 _87_	
Pay to the order of _Any Store_		$ _20.00_
Twenty and 00/100 ——————————————		Dollars
For _Shoes (on sale) for Mom_	_Jane Doe_	

The Check Register

The check register is a record of all the checks you have written and all the deposits you have made. It has six column headings. The first is "Number." In this space, you write the number of the check you have written. Those numbers come pre-printed, in order, in the upper right-hand corner of your checks.

The next column, "Date," is for the date that you write the check. Next is the "Description of Payments," which is where you record to whom you wrote the check (top line) and the reason you wrote it (bottom line). In the "Payment/Debit (-)" column, you write the amount of the check or a debit from the bank. A debit is when the bank charges you for such things as your box of checks, an overdraft charge, and so on.

The next column is "Deposit/Credit (+)." Here you will record the deposits you make or the credits the bank makes to your account. Such credits would be interest paid in certain kinds of checking accounts, corrections of bank mistakes, and so on. "Balance," the last column, is where you keep a running total of your checking account balance. This is so you know at all times how much money is in your account.

Here is a check register that has been filled out:

RECORD ALL CHARGES OR CREDITS THAT AFFECT YOUR ACCOUNT

NUMBER	DATE	DESCRIPTION OF TRANSACTION	PAYMENT/DEBIT (-)		√ T	FEE (if any) (-)	DEPOSIT/CREDIT (+)	BALANCE
								150 00
10	5/17	Any Store	- 20	00				- 20 00
		Gift for Mom						130 00

Check #10, dated May 17, was written to "Any Store" for a "gift for Mom." The check was for $20. The balance before the check was written was $150, so the new balance after the check is $130.

Filling out all the information on your check register is vitally important—you need to know where you stand financially at all times. It is also important that you record each check in your check register *at the time you write it*. If you don't, you may forget about it, and then your records will be wrong or incomplete. You may find out too late that you had less money than you thought and that you wrote one or more checks when your money was gone. This is called "overdrafting," and it costs you a penalty fee each time you do it.

8

Using a Checking Account with the Budget Booklet

Your check register and your Financial Freedom Junior Budget Booklet make a financially dynamic duo. You will use them together to wisely manage your money.

Let's suppose you have graduated from high school and that you are living and working away from home. You make $400 a month and get paid once a month. To keep things simple, let's say that you have only four budget categories: Housing, $150; Food, $160; Car, $50; Savings, $40. These add up to $400.

Monthly Paycheck

You deposit your monthly paycheck of $400 into your checking account and record that amount in your check register. Also, you write the four categories in your budget booklet, along with the amount you have budgeted to each. You place a check by the "Savings, $40" in your booklet and a check by the "balance forward" in your register. This is to remind yourself later that your register balance and your booklet balance are the same. This is called the Balancing Rule.

RECORD ALL CHARGES OR CREDITS THAT AFFECT YOUR ACCOUNT

NUMBER	DATE	DESCRIPTION OF TRANSACTION	PAYMENT/DEBIT (-)	√ T	FEE (if any) (-)	DEPOSIT/CREDIT (+)	BALANCE	
								00
	2/1	Paycheck				+400 00	+ 400	00
							400	00 √

February

Housing		Food		Car		Savings		
BUDGET	150.00	BUDGET	160.00	BUDGET	50.00	BUDGET	40.00	
ROLLOVER	—	ROLLOVER	—	ROLLOVER	—	ROLLOVER	—	√
BALANCE	150.00	BALANCE	160.00	BALANCE	50.00	BALANCE	40.00	400.00
Date / Check #		Date / Check #		Date / Check #		Date / Check #		
For / From		For / From		For / From		For / From		
Date / Check #		Date / Check #		Date / Check #		Date / Check #		
For / From		For / From		For / From		For / From		
Date / Check #		Date / Check #		Date / Check #		Date / Check #		
For / From		For / From		For / From		For / From		
Date / Check #		Date / Check #		Date / Check #		Date / Check #		
For / From		For / From		For / From		For / From		
Date / Check #		Date / Check #		Date / Check #		Date / Check #		
For / From		For / From		For / From		For / From		

Now it's time to pay your rent for the month. In your register, you write (1) the check number (#1), (2) the date (February 1), (3) to whom the money is paid, and (4) the purpose (February's rent). In the payment column, you write $150 (the amount of the check). Then in the balance column, you subtract $150 from the original $400, leaving a new bank balance of $250.

RECORD ALL CHARGES OR CREDITS THAT AFFECT YOUR ACCOUNT

NUMBER	DATE	DESCRIPTION OF TRANSACTION	PAYMENT/DEBIT (-)	√ T	FEE (if any) (-)	DEPOSIT/CREDIT (+)	BALANCE
							00
	2/1	Paycheck				+400 00	+ 400 00
							400 00 ✓
1	2/1	Landlord Jones	−150 00				− 150 00
		February's Rent					250 00

In your budget booklet, under the category of "Housing," you write (1) your check number, (2) your check amount ($150), and (3) your new housing balance ($0). You may also want to make a note of what the check was for.

February

Housing		Food		Car		Savings		
BUDGET	150.00	BUDGET	160.00	BUDGET	50.00	BUDGET	40.00	
ROLLOVER	—	ROLLOVER	—	ROLLOVER	—	ROLLOVER	—	✓
BALANCE	150.00	BALANCE	160.00	BALANCE	50.00	BALANCE	40.00	400.00
Date / Check # 1	−150.00	Date / Check #		Date / Check #		Date / Check #		
For / From Rent	.00	For / From		For / From		For / From		
Date / Check #		Date / Check #		Date / Check #		Date / Check #		
For / From		For / From		For / From		For / From		
Date / Check #		Date / Check #		Date / Check #		Date / Check #		
For / From		For / From		For / From		For / From		
Date / Check #		Date / Check #		Date / Check #		Date / Check #		
For / From		For / From		For / From		For / From		
Date / Check #		Date / Check #		Date / Check #		Date / Check #		
For / From		For / From		For / From		For / From		

Next, you go to the grocery store and spend $15.50. You write the entry in your check register and bring down your new bank balance of $234.50.

NUMBER	DATE	DESCRIPTION OF TRANSACTION	PAYMENT/DEBIT (-)	√ T	FEE (if any) (-)	DEPOSIT/CREDIT (+)	BALANCE	
		RECORD ALL CHARGES OR CREDITS THAT AFFECT YOUR ACCOUNT						00
	2/1	Paycheck				+400 00	+400 00 400 00	√
1	2/1	Landlord Jones February's Rent	-150 00				-150 00 250 00	
2	2/3	Grocery Store	-15 50				-15 50 234 50	

You then write the entry in your budget booklet under the "Food" category. Your new food balance is $144.50. You do all this while you are still in the store. That way you won't forget to do it later.

February

Housing		Food		Car		Savings		
BUDGET	150.00	BUDGET	160.00	BUDGET	50.00	BUDGET	40.00	
ROLLOVER	—	ROLLOVER	—	ROLLOVER	—	ROLLOVER	—	√
BALANCE	150.00	BALANCE	160.00	BALANCE	50.00	BALANCE	40.00	400.00
Date / Check # 1	-150.00	Date / Check # 2	-15.50	Date / Check #		Date / Check #		
For / From Rent	.00	For / From Store	144.50	For / From		For / From		
Date / Check #		Date / Check #		Date / Check #		Date / Check #		
For / From		For / From		For / From		For / From		
Date / Check #		Date / Check #		Date / Check #		Date / Check #		
For / From		For / From		For / From		For / From		
Date / Check #		Date / Check #		Date / Check #		Date / Check #		
For / From		For / From		For / From		For / From		
Date / Check #		Date / Check #		Date / Check #		Date / Check #		
For / From		For / From		For / From		For / From		

Your third check goes to buy $12 worth of gas. You record the purchase in your register, giving you a new balance of $222.50. You enter the purchase in your booklet, for a new "Car" balance of $38. You do all this right at the gas station. There is no "homework" with this system, because you keep it current as you go.

RECORD ALL CHARGES OR CREDITS THAT AFFECT YOUR ACCOUNT

NUMBER	DATE	DESCRIPTION OF TRANSACTION	PAYMENT/DEBIT (-)	√ T	FEE (If any) (-)	DEPOSIT/CREDIT (+)	BALANCE	
								00
	2/1	Paycheck				+400 00	+ 400	00
							400	00 √
1	2/1	Landlord Jones February's Rent	- 150 00				- 150	00
							250	00
2	2/3	Grocery Store	- 15 50				- 15	50
							234	50
3	2/6	Jay's Station Gas	- 12 00				- 12	00
							222	50

February

Housing		Food		Car		Savings	
BUDGET	150.00	BUDGET	160.00	BUDGET	50.00	BUDGET	40.00
ROLLOVER	—	ROLLOVER	—	ROLLOVER	—	ROLLOVER	—
BALANCE	150.00	BALANCE	160.00	BALANCE	50.00	BALANCE	40.00
Date / Check # 1	-150.00	Date / Check # 2	- 15.50	Date / Check # 3	-12.00	Date / Check #	
For / From Rent	.00	For / From Store	144.50	For / From Gas	38.00	For / From	
Date / Check #		Date / Check #		Date / Check #		Date / Check #	
For / From		For / From		For / From		For / From	
Date / Check #		Date / Check #		Date / Check #		Date / Check #	
For / From		For / From		For / From		For / From	
Date / Check #		Date / Check #		Date / Check #		Date / Check #	
For / From		For / From		For / From		For / From	
Date / Check #		Date / Check #		Date / Check #		Date / Check #	
For / From		For / From		For / From		For / From	

√ 400.00

Your birthday comes during the month and, among other presents, you receive a gift of $25 cash. You deposit it in your checking account, for a new register balance of $247.50. You next enter it in your booklet in the savings category. Good for you! Your new balance there is now $65. (You could have budgeted it anywhere else, of course.) Instead of writing in a check number, you write in the date (February 11) you enter the deposit into your booklet.

RECORD ALL CHARGES OR CREDITS THAT AFFECT YOUR ACCOUNT

NUMBER	DATE	DESCRIPTION OF TRANSACTION	PAYMENT/DEBIT (-)	√ T	FEE (if any) (-)	DEPOSIT/CREDIT (+)	BALANCE	
								00
	2/1	Paycheck				+400 00	+400	00
							400	00 √
1	2/1	Landlord Jones February's Rent	- 150 00				- 150	00
							250	00
2	2/3	Grocery Store	- 15 50				- 15	50
							234	50
3	2/6	Jay's Station Gas	- 12 00				- 12	00
							222	50
	2/11	Birthday Gift My Sister				+ 25 00	+ 25	00
							247	50

February

Housing		Food		Car		Savings		
BUDGET	150.00	BUDGET	160.00	BUDGET	50.00	BUDGET	40.00	
ROLLOVER	—	ROLLOVER	—	ROLLOVER	—	ROLLOVER	—	√
BALANCE	150.00	BALANCE	160.00	BALANCE	50.00	BALANCE	40.00	400.00
Date / Check # 1	-150.00	Date / Check # 2	- 15.50	Date / Check # 3	-12.00	Date / Check # 2/11	+ 25.00	
For / From Rent	.00	For / From Store	144.50	For / From Gas	38.00	For / From Gift	65.00	
Date / Check #		Date / Check #		Date / Check #		Date / Check #		
For / From		For / From		For / From		For / From		
Date / Check #		Date / Check #		Date / Check #		Date / Check #		
For / From		For / From		For / From		For / From		
Date / Check #		Date / Check #		Date / Check #		Date / Check #		
For / From		For / From		For / From		For / From		
Date / Check #		Date / Check #		Date / Check #		Date / Check #		
For / From		For / From		For / From		For / From		

Your bank charges you a $3 service charge in February, which you don't know about until your bank statement comes. You enter the $3 charge in your register just like a check, except that you write a dash in the "Check No." space, since the charge was deducted from your account by the bank—you didn't write a check for it. Your new register balance is $244.50. In your booklet, you subtract the charge from your savings category just as you would have for a check. Again, instead of the check number, you write in the date (February 11). Your new savings balance is $62.

RECORD ALL CHARGES OR CREDITS THAT AFFECT YOUR ACCOUNT

NUMBER	DATE	DESCRIPTION OF TRANSACTION	PAYMENT/DEBIT (-)	√ T	FEE (if any) (-)	DEPOSIT/CREDIT (+)	BALANCE	00
	2/1	Paycheck				+400 00	+400 00	
							400 00	√
1	2/1	Landlord Jones February's Rent	-150 00				-150 00	
							250 00	
2	2/3	Grocery Store	-15 50				-15 50	
							234 50	
3	2/6	Jay's Station Gas	-12 00				-12 00	
							222 50	
	2/11	Birthday Gift My Sister				+25 00	+25 00	
							247 50	
—	2/11	Bank Service Charge	-3 00				-3 00	
							244 50	

February

Housing		Food		Car		Savings	
BUDGET	150.00	BUDGET	160.00	BUDGET	50.00	BUDGET	40.00
ROLLOVER	—	ROLLOVER	—	ROLLOVER	—	ROLLOVER	—
BALANCE	150.00	BALANCE	160.00	BALANCE	50.00	BALANCE	40.00
Date / Check # 1	-150.00	Date / Check # 2	-15.50	Date / Check # 3	-12.00	Date / Check # 2/11	+25.00
For / From Rent	.00	For / From Store	144.50	For / From Gas	38.00	For / From Gift	65.00
Date / Check #		Date / Check #		Date / Check #		Date / Check # 2/11	-3.00
For / From		For / From		For / From		For / From Bk. Chg.	62.00
Date / Check #		Date / Check #		Date / Check #		Date / Check #	
For / From		For / From		For / From		For / From	
Date / Check #		Date / Check #		Date / Check #		Date / Check #	
For / From		For / From		For / From		For / From	
Date / Check #		Date / Check #		Date / Check #		Date / Check #	
For / From		For / From		For / From		For / From	

√ 400.00

You write four more checks that month, and you enter all four in both your register and your booklet, as shown in the illustration below. As a result, at the end of February, your month-end register balance is $67.67, and your booklet balances were: Housing = $0; Food = $(2.33); Car = $8; and Savings = $62.

Just as you did a beginning-of-the-month balance, you do an end-of-the-month balance. (Because the food category balance was negative, you subtracted the $2.33 from your category balances instead of adding it.) You put check marks by your register balance of $67.67 and by the total of your booklet balances of $67.67, to show that your accounts balance.

RECORD ALL CHARGES OR CREDITS THAT AFFECT YOUR ACCOUNT

NUMBER	DATE	DESCRIPTION OF TRANSACTION	PAYMENT/DEBIT (-)	√ T	FEE (if any) (-)	DEPOSIT/CREDIT (+)	BALANCE
							00
	2/1	Paycheck				+400 00	+400 00
							400 00 √
1	2/1	Landlord Jones February's Rent	-150 00				-150 00
							250 00
2	2/3	Grocery Store	-15 50				-15 50
							234 50
3	2/6	Jay's Station Gas	-12 00				-12 00
							222 50
	2/11	Birthday Gift				+25 00	+25 00
							247 50
—	2/11	Bank Service Charge	-3 00				-3 00
							244 50

RECORD ALL CHARGES OR CREDITS THAT AFFECT YOUR ACCOUNT

NUMBER	DATE	DESCRIPTION OF TRANSACTION	PAYMENT/DEBIT (-)	√ T	FEE (if any) (-)	DEPOSIT/CREDIT (+)	BALANCE
4	2/13	Grocery Store	-121 60				-121 60
							122 90
5	2/19	Jay's Station Gas	-16 00				-16 00
							106 90
6	2/25	Jay's Station Gas	-14 00				-14 00
							92 90
7	2/28	Grocery Store	-25 23				-25 23
							67 67 √

February

Housing		Food		Car		Savings		
BUDGET	150.00	BUDGET	160.00	BUDGET	50.00	BUDGET	40.00	
ROLLOVER	—	ROLLOVER	—	ROLLOVER	—	ROLLOVER	—	✓
BALANCE	150.00	BALANCE	160.00	BALANCE	50.00	BALANCE	40.00	400.00
Date / Check # 1	-150.00	Date / Check # 2	-15.50	Date / Check # 3	-12.00	Date / Check # 2/11	+25.00	
For / From Rent	.00	For / From Store	144.50	For / From Gas	38.00	For / From Gift	65.00	
Date / Check #		Date / Check # 4	-121.60	Date / Check # 5	-16.00	Date / Check # 2/11	-3.00	
For / From		For / From Store	22.90	For / From Gas	22.00	For / From Bk. Chg.	62.00	
Date / Check #		Date / Check # 7	-25.23	Date / Check # 6	-14.00	Date / Check #		
For / From		For / From Store	(2.33)	For / From Gas	8.00	For / From		
Date / Check #		Date / Check #		Date / Check #		Date / Check #		
For / From		For / From		For / From		For / From		
Date / Check #		Date / Check #		Date / Check #		Date / Check #		
For / From	0	For / From	(2.33)	For / From	8.00	For / From	62.00	✓ 67.67

As we said, the parentheses around the $2.33 in your food balance means you overspent your food category by that much. You had four choices at the time you made that purchase:

1. You could have increased your food budget by $2.33 and decreased some other category budget by $2.33. We recommend that you do not do that. Instead, if you possibly can, wait until you have lived with your budget for at least ninety days. After that, you may see a trend that means you should adjust your budget amounts.

2. You could have shifted $2.33 from one or more of your other category balances. We recommend that you do not do that, either. Once you start shifting, it is too easy to develop a habit of doing it, in any category, and soon your category balances mean nothing because you just keep shifting money from one to another.

3. You could have decided not to overspend the $2.33. Two of the greatest advantages to your booklet are that it goes where you go when you spend money, and it tells you exactly how much money you have left in any category. With that kind of on-the-spot information, you

could have bought $2.33 less worth of food and stayed within your budgeted amount.

4. You could have given yourself an advance of $2.33 from your next month's food category, which is exactly what you did by having a negative amount (-2.33) in your food category. This means that next month you will start with $2.33 in the hole.

You received your monthly paycheck for March and deposited it in your checking account. In your register, you wrote in that $400 deposit and added it to your register balance of $67.67, which gave you a new beginning-of-the-month register balance of $467.67.

You got out a new booklet for March and wrote in the same four categories you used in February. You then wrote the same monthly budget figures or percentages as last month, for each of the four categories.

The Rollover

The "rollover" is the money you have left over (or are short, as in your food category) at the end of the month in each category. You add (or subtract) the rollover money to your budget amounts in the new month—a simple procedure.

For example, you copied the month-end balance from each category in your February booklet to the line labeled "Rollover" in each category in your March booklet. You had no money left in "housing" from February, so you wrote $0 on the rollover line under "Housing" in March. You had a $2.33 shortage in "Food," so you wrote $(2.33) on the rollover line under "Food." (Parentheses are used to show a negative balance.) You had $8 left in gas, so you wrote that figure under gas. You had $62 left in savings, which you carried over to savings for March.

You then added the totals in each budget category to

the positive figures on each rollover line under "Housing," "Car," and "Savings." Under "Food," you subtracted the rollover line negative balance from the budgeted amount. That gave you your new beginning balances in each category for March. (You started the new month with $2.33 less than your monthly food budget because you advanced yourself that $2.33 last month when you overspent that category.)

You then did your beginning-of-the-month balance for March. You added across all four of your beginning figures under each category in your March booklet for a total of $467.67. You compared that with your register balance of $467.67 to see that your accounts were balanced.

RECORD ALL CHARGES OR CREDITS THAT AFFECT YOUR ACCOUNT

NUMBER	DATE	DESCRIPTION OF TRANSACTION	PAYMENT/DEBIT (-)	√ T	FEE (if any) (-)	DEPOSIT/CREDIT (+)	BALANCE 00
	2/1	Paycheck				+400 00	+ 400 00 400 00 √
1	2/1	Landlord Jones February's Rent	-150 00				- 150 00 250 00
2	2/3	Grocery Store	-15 50				- 15 50 234 50
3	2/6	Jay's Station Gas	-12 00				- 12 00 222 50
	2/11	Birthday Gift My Sister				+25 00	+ 25 00 247 50
—	2/11	Bank Service Charge	- 3 00				- 3 00 244 50

RECORD ALL CHARGES OR CREDITS THAT AFFECT YOUR ACCOUNT

NUMBER	DATE	DESCRIPTION OF TRANSACTION	PAYMENT/DEBIT (-)	√ T	FEE (if any) (-)	DEPOSIT/CREDIT (+)	BALANCE
4	2/13	Grocery Store	-121 60				- 121 60 122 90
5	2/19	Jay's Station Gas	-16 00				- 16 00 106 90
6	2/25	Jay's Station Gas	-14 00				- 14 00 92 90
7	2/28	Grocery Store	-25 23				- 25 23 67 67 √
	3/1					+400 00	+ 400 00 467 67 √

March

Housing		Food		Car		Savings		
BUDGET	150.00	BUDGET	160.00	BUDGET	50.00	BUDGET	40.00	
ROLLOVER	.00	ROLLOVER	(2.33)	ROLLOVER	8.00	ROLLOVER	62.00	✓
BALANCE	150.00	BALANCE	157.67	BALANCE	58.00	BALANCE	102.00	467.67
Date / Check #		Date / Check #		Date / Check #		Date / Check #		
For / From		For / From		For / From		For / From		
Date / Check #		Date / Check #		Date / Check #		Date / Check #		
For / From		For / From		For / From		For / From		
Date / Check #		Date / Check #		Date / Check #		Date / Check #		
For / From		For / From		For / From		For / From		
Date / Check #		Date / Check #		Date / Check #		Date / Check #		
For / From		For / From		For / From		For / From		
Date / Check #		Date / Check #		Date / Check #		Date / Check #		
For / From		For / From		For / From		For / From		

You were then through with your February booklet, so you stored it for historical or income-tax purposes. You slipped your March booklet into your register cover, and you were ready to spend in the new month.

Each budget booklet is ordinarily used for one month. However, some people prefer to use one booklet for each paycheck, which could be two or four per month. Others use the same booklet for two months. This does not mean that they balance their accounts only once every two months. They just do the balancing in the same booklet, marking the date they balanced. Then they continue spending for the next month but using the same booklet.

Two Paychecks a Month

On the budget booklet cover are two income columns—one labeled "First Paycheck" and the other labeled "Second Paycheck." You can use these columns to divide up your monthly budget amounts that you will spend from each of your two paychecks.

Again referring to our example, let us say that you

budgeted all $150 of your housing money from your first paycheck because your rent payment is due by the fifth of the month. You wrote $150 under "First Paycheck," next to "Housing." You then subtracted the $150 you just budgeted to housing from your total "First Paycheck" amount of $200, giving you $50 left to budget for the first half of the month. Of that $50, you decided to budget $35 to food. You wrote $35 under "First Paycheck" next to "Food." You subtracted $35 from the $50 you had left, which gave you $15 to budget for your two remaining categories for the first half of the month. You then decided to budget all $15 to "Car." So, you wrote $15 next to "Car" under "First Paycheck." There was nothing left to budget to savings, so you wrote a zero on that line under "First Paycheck."

Next, you added up your budget amounts under "First Paycheck" to make sure that the total equaled the amount of your first paycheck. You then wrote in $200 on the "Subtotals" lines under "First Paycheck."

CATEGORY	FIRST PAYCHECK	SECOND PAYCHECK	CATEGORY	FIRST PAYCHECK	SECOND PAYCHECK
1. Housing	150.00		11.		
2. Food	35.00		12.		
3. Car	15.00		13.		
4. Savings	.00		14.		
5.			15.		
6.			16.		
7.			17.		
8.			18.		
9.			19.		
10.			20.		

NAME _____ MONTH _____ YEAR _____   TOTAL 200.00 _____

Then you repeated the planning procedure for your second paycheck. You wrote zero on the "Housing" line under "Second Paycheck" because you paid your entire rent from your first paycheck. You subtracted $35 of "Food" under "First Paycheck" from your total food budget of $160, and you wrote in the $125 you had left from "Second Paycheck" for food. Next, you subtracted the $15 for "Car" under "First Paycheck" from your total car budget of $50. The remainder to budget for your car for the last half of the month was $35, which you wrote under "Second Paycheck." You then wrote all $40 of your savings money on that line under "Second Paycheck."

To check your arithmetic, you added your budgeted amounts under "Second Paycheck" to make sure the amount was the same as your second paycheck amount. It was, so you wrote in $200 on the "Subtotals" line under "Second Paycheck."

CATEGORY	FIRST PAYCHECK	SECOND PAYCHECK		CATEGORY	FIRST PAYCHECK	SECOND PAYCHECK
1. Housing	150.00	.00	11.			
2. Food	35.00	125.00	12.			
3. Car	15.00	35.00	13.			
4. Savings	.00	40.00	14.			
5.			15.			
6.			16.			
7.			17.			
8.			18.			
9.			19.			
10.			20.			

NAME _____ MONTH _____ YEAR _____   TOTAL 200.00 200.00

Next, you copied your four budget categories from your booklet cover to the category columns inside your booklet. You then looked on the booklet cover again, this time to see how much you budgeted for each of those four categories from your first paycheck. You entered those amounts in the budget spaces under the category titles inside your booklet: $150 under "Housing", $35 under "Food", $15 under "Car" and $0 under "Savings."

February

Housing		Food		Car		Savings	
BUDGET		BUDGET		BUDGET		BUDGET	
ROLLOVER		ROLLOVER		ROLLOVER		ROLLOVER	
BALANCE	150.00	BALANCE	35.00	BALANCE	15.00	BALANCE	.00
Date / Check #		Date / Check #		Date / Check #		Date / Check #	
For / From		For / From		For / From		For / From	
Date / Check #		Date / Check #		Date / Check #		Date / Check #	
For / From		For / From		For / From		For / From	
Date / Check #		Date / Check #		Date / Check #		Date / Check #	
For / From		For / From		For / From		For / From	
Date / Check #		Date / Check #		Date / Check #		Date / Check #	
For / From		For / From		For / From		For / From	
Date / Check #		Date / Check #		Date / Check #		Date / Check #	
For / From		For / From		For / From		For / From	

Just as you did in our first example, you then deposited your first paycheck in your checking account. Then you spent your money according to your plan.

You spent check number 1 for $150 for housing, leaving a balance of $50. Then you spent $31.75 on food, using check number 2, leaving $3.25 in your food budget. You spent $15.00 for gasoline for your car.

RECORD ALL CHARGES OR CREDITS THAT AFFECT YOUR ACCOUNT

NUMBER	DATE	DESCRIPTION OF TRANSACTION	PAYMENT/DEBIT (-)	√ T	FEE (if any) (-)	DEPOSIT/CREDIT (+)	BALANCE	
								00
	2/1	Paycheck				+200 00	+ 200	00
							200	00
1	2/1	Landlord Jones	-150 00				-150	00
		February Rent					50	00
2	2/5	Grocery Store	- 31 75				- 31	75
		Food					18	25
3	2/9	Jim's Service	-15 00				- 15	00
		Gas					3	25

February

Housing		Food		Car		Savings	
BUDGET		BUDGET		BUDGET		BUDGET	
ROLLOVER		ROLLOVER		ROLLOVER		ROLLOVER	
BALANCE	150.00	BALANCE	35.00	BALANCE	15.00	BALANCE	.00
Date / Check # 1	-150.00	Date / Check # 2	-31.75	Date / Check # 3	-15.00	Date / Check #	
For / From Rent	.00	For / From Food	3.25	For / From Gas	.00	For / From	
Date / Check #		Date / Check #		Date / Check #		Date / Check #	
For / From		For / From		For / From		For / From	
Date / Check #		Date / Check #		Date / Check #		Date / Check #	
For / From		For / From		For / From		For / From	
Date / Check #		Date / Check #		Date / Check #		Date / Check #	
For / From		For / From		For / From		For / From	
Date / Check #		Date / Check #		Date / Check #		Date / Check #	
For / From		For / From		For / From		For / From	
Date / Check #		Date / Check #		Date / Check #		Date / Check #	
For / From		For / From		For / From		For / From	

You received your second paycheck for the month and deposited it, recording it in your check register. That gave you a new register balance of $203.25 (from the new $200 paycheck and the $3.25 left in your register).

RECORD ALL CHARGES OR CREDITS THAT AFFECT YOUR ACCOUNT

NUMBER	DATE	DESCRIPTION OF TRANSACTION	PAYMENT/DEBIT (-)	√ T	FEE (if any) (-)	DEPOSIT/CREDIT (+)	BALANCE	
								00
	2/1	Paycheck				+200 00	+ 200	00
							200	00
1	2/1	Landlord Jones February Rent	-150 00				-150	00
							50	00
2	2/5	Grocery Store Food	-31 75				- 31	75
							.18	25
3	2/9	Jim's Service Gas	-15 00				-' 15	00
							3	25
	2/15	Paycheck				+200 00	+200	00
							203	25

You then recorded the budget amounts in your booklet. From the cover of your booklet, under "Second Paycheck," you copied inside your booklet $0 for housing, $125 for food, $35 for car, and $40 for savings. You recorded each of these amounts in the appropriate columns of your budget book right under your last transactions, using a plus mark to show that the amounts came from a deposit to your checking account. Then you added these amounts to your remaining balances, which were all $0 except for the $3.25 balance left in your food budget.

You then added your "what's-left" figures in each budget category to the new mid-month figures you just entered in each category. Your new housing balance was still zero because you didn't put any more money in that category. The food category had $3.25 left, which you added to the mid-month entry of $125 for a new total of $128.25. Your car category had nothing left, so the new $35 was the mid-month total. You put $40 in savings, which added to zero, is $40.

February

Housing		Food		Car		Savings	
BUDGET		BUDGET		BUDGET		BUDGET	
ROLLOVER		ROLLOVER		ROLLOVER		ROLLOVER	
BALANCE	150.00	BALANCE	35.00	BALANCE	15.00	BALANCE	.00
Date/Check# 1	-150.00	Date/Check# 2	-31.75	Date/Check# 3	-15.00	Date/Check# 2/15	+40.00
For/From Rent	.00	For/From Food	3.25	For/From Gas	.00	For/From Paycheck	40.00
Date/Check#		Date/Check# 2/15	+125.00	Date/Check# 2/15	+35.00	Date/Check#	
For/From		For/From Paycheck	128.25	For/From Paycheck	35.00	For/From	
Date/Check#		Date/Check#		Date/Check#		Date/Check#	
For/From		For/From		For/From		For/From	
Date/Check#		Date/Check#		Date/Check#		Date/Check#	
For/From		For/From		For/From		For/From	
Date/Check#		Date/Check#		Date/Check#		Date/Check#	
For/From		For/From		For/From		For/From	

You did a mid-month balancing by adding your four category totals ($203.25) and checking them against your register total ($203.25). From that point on, the procedure is the same as for one paycheck per month.

Some people who get paid twice a month use two booklets per month instead of making the mid-month entries in the same booklet. That means, of course, that they do everything in the middle of the month (end balance, rollover, and so on) that they would normally do at the end of a month. Choose the method you like best.

Weekly Paychecks

If you are paid weekly, you can follow the two-paycheck method, only you would repeat the procedures weekly instead of just once in the middle of the month, using the same booklet for a month. Or, you might consider using a new booklet each week, doing your balancing, rollover, and so on every week.

9

Your Financial Future

Some time ago, a group of teenagers from a local high-school newspaper came to interview us about our book *Rich on Any Income*. They came, not knowing we were writing a book for young people, to talk about financial matters of importance to youth, now and in the future. They wrote a fine article called "Budgets Are the Key to Financial Stability for Teens." Here are some of the things they said:

"Many people think budgets are only for the government or busy housewives, but more and more they are discovering that's just not so. Budgets are good for anybody."

"You won't financially exist without a budget."

"Putting together a monthly budget is simple and takes a minimal amount of time."

"As the needs change, budgets can change. Spending habits will change, and so will the spending categories, especially after high school."

"If a person invested $2,000 a year in an Individual Retirement Account from the time he or she was twenty-three, that person could retire at age sixty-five with more than one million dollars in savings!"

It has been interesting for us as we travel around the country to learn that people of all ages are very concerned about their financial future. In this book, we have taken you from home bank to savings account to checking account. As you "graduate" from these "courses," you will still need answers to many important questions about your financial future, such as:

"Should I get a credit card? Should I get more than one? How much interest will I have to pay?"

"What is an installment loan? How do I know if one is right for me?"

"What about home loans? What is amortization?"

"What does consolidation of debts mean? What is refinancing? What does home equity mean?"

"How much can I invest each year in an Individual Retirement Account?"

About now, one of your questions is probably "Where can I learn the answers to these questions?" The answers to most of those questions are in our book *Rich on Any Income*. It teaches more about a checking account, using credit cards, and many other financial subjects. So, when you graduate from this junior plan, give yourself a graduation present and get the senior plan, *Rich on Any Income*.

If you have read this whole book, you have taken the first step to becoming financially free. You have learned how to open and maintain a savings account and a checking account. You have learned how to budget your money and how to save money. You have learned how to use the best money management tool available, the Financial Freedom Junior Budget Booklet, with both cash and a checking account. You have read the testimonials of young people who have been on the Financial Freedom Budget System, and you have learned what it has done for them. It can do the same for you.

You now have the knowledge and skills necessary to stay out of unwanted debt and to live within your means for the rest of your life. You have within your reach financial happiness and peace of mind.

The only thing left for you to do now to be successful is to make a commitment. Commit right now to manage your money well throughout your life.

This is our promise: If you will faithfully follow the principles and procedures taught in this book, you can have more of anything you want financially as long as you plan for it with enough work and time. Good luck and good spending!

Budget Booklet

Here is your copy of the Financial Freedom Junior Budget Booklet. To assemble this booklet, cut the pages from this book along the dotted lines. This will give you three loose pages. Take the pages, labeled A, B, and C in the lower right-hand corner. With the letters A, B, and C right-side up and facing up, put these three sheets on top of each other. Put the A sheet on the table first; then put the B sheet on top of the A sheet; finally, put the C sheet on top of the B sheet. Line up the staple marks in the center of the three sheets. Staple the sheets together along the center where the two staple marks appear. Finally, fold the top half of the booklet forward along the staple marks. More budget booklets, already assembled, can be ordered using the form on the cover of the budget booklet included in this book.

FINANCIAL FREEDOM
JUNIOR
BUDGET BOOKLET

The Easy Budgeting System for Kids and Teens

CATEGORY	FIRST PAYCHECK	SECOND PAYCHECK		CATEGORY	FIRST PAYCHECK	SECOND PAYCHECK
1.				11.		
2.				12.		
3.				13.		
4.				14.		
5.				15.		
6.				16.		
7.				17.		
8.				18.		
9.				19.		
10.				20.		

NAME _____ MONTH _____ YEAR _____ TOTAL _____

BUDGET		BUDGET		BUDGET	
ROLLOVER		ROLLOVER		ROLLOVER	
BALANCE		BALANCE		BALANCE	
Date / Check #		Date / Check #		Date / Check #	
For / From		For / From		For / From	
Date / Check #		Date / Check #		Date / Check #	
For / From		For / From		For / From	
Date / Check #		Date / Check #		Date / Check #	
For / From		For / From		For / From	
Date / Check #		Date / Check #		Date / Check #	
For / From		For / From		For / From	
Date / Check #		Date / Check #		Date / Check #	
For / From		For / From		For / From	
Date / Check #		Date / Check #		Date / Check #	
For / From		For / From		For / From	

To order a 12-month supply of the Financial Freedom Junior Budget Booklet or the book *Rich on Any Allowance: The Easy Budgeting System for Kids and Teens*, call one of the toll-free numbers or mail your order today.

PHONE ORDERS:
(Credit card customers only)

Outside Utah call toll free
1-800-453-4532

In Utah call toll free
1-800-662-3653

Local calls 534-1515

For information about a seminar on the Financial Freedom Junior Budgeting System for your group, organization, or conference, contact: Deseret Book, Attn: Financial Freedom Budget Seminars, P.O. Box 30178, Salt Lake City, Utah 84130.

Deseret Book
EXPRESS

For a complete explanation of how to use the Financial Freedom Junior Budgeting System (of which this booklet is a part), you'll want to read *Rich on Any Allowance: The Easy Budgeting System for Kids and Teens*.

MAIL ORDERS:
Mail to: Deseret Book Express. P.O. Box 30178, Salt Lake City, Utah 84130

	Quan	Price	Total
Financial Freedom Junior Budget Booklet (12 booklets)		$10.00	
Rich on Any Allowance		$8.95	
Rich on Any Income (For adults) . . .		$8.95	
Subtotal			
Sales tax (where applicable) (For orders being shipped to the following states, add appropriate sales tax: Utah 5³/₄%, California 6%, Idaho 4%.)			
Total (No additional postage or handling required.)			

☐ Check enclosed ☐ VISA ☐ MasterCard ☐ American Express

Card # _____ Exp. date _____

Name _____

Address _____

H8

BUDGET		
ROLLOVER		
BALANCE		
Date / Check #	Date / Check #	Date / Check #
For / From	For / From	For / From
Date / Check #	Date / Check #	Date / Check #
For / From	For / From	For / From
Date / Check #	Date / Check #	Date / Check #
For / From	For / From	For / From
Date / Check #	Date / Check #	Date / Check #
For / From	For / From	For / From
Date / Check #	Date / Check #	Date / Check #
For / From	For / From	For / From

BUDGET		
ROLLOVER		
BALANCE		
Date / Check #	Date / Check #	Date / Check #
For / From	For / From	For / From
Date / Check #	Date / Check #	Date / Check #
For / From	For / From	For / From
Date / Check #	Date / Check #	Date / Check #
For / From	For / From	For / From
Date / Check #	Date / Check #	Date / Check #
For / From	For / From	For / From
Date / Check #	Date / Check #	Date / Check #
For / From	For / From	For / From

(b)

BUDGET
ROLLOVER
BALANCE

Date / Check #	
For / From	
Date / Check #	
For / From	
Date / Check #	
For / From	
Date / Check #	
For / From	
Date / Check #	
For / From	
Date / Check #	
For / From	
Date / Check #	
For / From	
Date / Check #	
For / From	
Date / Check #	
For / From	

BUDGET
ROLLOVER
BALANCE

Date / Check #	
For / From	
Date / Check #	
For / From	
Date / Check #	
For / From	
Date / Check #	
For / From	
Date / Check #	
For / From	
Date / Check #	
For / From	
Date / Check #	
For / From	
Date / Check #	
For / From	
Date / Check #	
For / From	

BUDGET
ROLLOVER
BALANCE

Date / Check #	
For / From	
Date / Check #	
For / From	
Date / Check #	
For / From	
Date / Check #	
For / From	
Date / Check #	
For / From	
Date / Check #	
For / From	
Date / Check #	
For / From	
Date / Check #	
For / From	
Date / Check #	
For / From	

BUDGET
ROLLOVER
BALANCE

Date / Check #	
For / From	
Date / Check #	
For / From	
Date / Check #	
For / From	
Date / Check #	
For / From	
Date / Check #	
For / From	
Date / Check #	
For / From	
Date / Check #	
For / From	
Date / Check #	
For / From	
Date / Check #	
For / From	

BUDGET	
ROLLOVER	
BALANCE	
Date / Check #	
For / From	
Date / Check #	
For / From	
Date / Check #	
For / From	
Date / Check #	
For / From	
Date / Check #	
For / From	
Date / Check #	
For / From	
Date / Check #	
For / From	

BUDGET	
ROLLOVER	
BALANCE	
Date / Check #	
For / From	
Date / Check #	
For / From	
Date / Check #	
For / From	
Date / Check #	
For / From	
Date / Check #	
For / From	
Date / Check #	
For / From	
Date / Check #	
For / From	

BUDGET	
ROLLOVER	
BALANCE	
Date / Check #	
For / From	
Date / Check #	
For / From	
Date / Check #	
For / From	
Date / Check #	
For / From	
Date / Check #	
For / From	
Date / Check #	
For / From	
Date / Check #	
For / From	

BUDGET	
ROLLOVER	
BALANCE	
Date / Check #	
For / From	
Date / Check #	
For / From	
Date / Check #	
For / From	
Date / Check #	
For / From	
Date / Check #	
For / From	
Date / Check #	
For / From	
Date / Check #	
For / From	

(c)

BUDGET	
ROLLOVER	
BALANCE	
For / From	
Date / Check #	
For / From	
Date / Check #	
For / From	
Date / Check #	
For / From	
Date / Check #	
For / From	
Date / Check #	
For / From	
Date / Check #	
For / From	

BUDGET	
ROLLOVER	
BALANCE	
For / From	
Date / Check #	
For / From	
Date / Check #	
For / From	
Date / Check #	
For / From	
Date / Check #	
For / From	
Date / Check #	
For / From	
Date / Check #	
For / From	

BUDGET	
ROLLOVER	
BALANCE	
For / From	
Date / Check #	
For / From	
Date / Check #	
For / From	
Date / Check #	
For / From	
Date / Check #	
For / From	
Date / Check #	
For / From	
Date / Check #	
For / From